To Judi,
hope you
J Steve

IT'S ALL ABOUT YOU

Stephen J Ellis

www.
BooksOfKnowledge
.co.uk

IT'S ALL ABOUT YOU

ISBN 978-0-9555370-0-4

First Edition, February 2007
Published by Books of Knowledge

Printed in Great Britain for Books of Knowledge by
Biddles Ltd., King's Lynn, Norfolk PE30 4LS.

IT'S ALL ABOUT YOU

To all the inspirational people in my life, a big thank-you for all the help, love, support and understanding I receive from you.

To Sam - my editor, wife, friend, guide, and love - I couldn't have done it without you.

Love, Steve x x

It's All About You

Stephen J Ellis

INTRODUCTION

'It's All About You' in essence becomes 'It's All About Me' as soon as it's picked up to read. So congratulations, by choosing this Book you've already begun to choose yourself. It is a Book that wants to guide and inspire you upon a path of personal development and self-discovery. Maybe this is why you've bought a copy. Whatever the motive, for many it takes courage and determination, because in our society this journey can mistakenly be construed as selfish, or only for the self-absorbed. But what's the harm in snuggling up a little closer to ourselves?

I work as a complementary therapist, and when recounting the title of my draft manuscript to a colleague, she immediately exclaimed, "a carpet salesman told me last night, 'it's not **all** about you', so I immediately replied, 'who **is** it about then?'" It appears she was very clear on her preferences, which seemingly conflicted with the salesman's ideas of what she might like, and so his inappropriate interjection was clearly designed to wrest control from my colleague in order to steer her into the sale he wanted for her. Unless we know ourselves and can stand firm against such intrusions, others can readily take advantage – but only if we let them.

So yes, it **is** all about you. I settled upon this title, for one central reason. I believe it conveys a simple message that is central to any personal development theme, which is the most important relationship you will ever have in your life is the one with yourself. How you value yourself will determine how your life turns out, because all your other relationships depend on the quality of your self-relationship; so it's vital to get it working with and for you.

We all want to be happy, and undoubtedly the key to happiness is to be found in loving relationships. Of course a level of happiness can be found in the material world, and it plays an important role in our lives; but if your emotional world isn't ticking along to a certain extent everything else becomes devalued, sometimes even meaningless.

Our self-esteem relies upon us meeting our goals, by feeling proud of our achievements and worthy because of our deeds. The cornerstone of positive motivation is unconditional love; but seemingly, either because of our education system or the traditional values found in our society, British people appear rather more adept at conferring unconditional love on everybody else than on themselves. Tolerance plays a big part in the national psyche and we are a welcoming nation, but we don't always extend this welcome to ourselves; we can often be our worst critics, when surely we should be our best friends?

In what can sometimes seem to be a 'don't care' world it is easy to also fall into this way of thinking about ourselves. The power of negative thinking is to make us believe it is the only game in town and that we couldn't change even if we wanted to. 'It's All About You' seeks to light the touch paper that ignites the latent self-relationship. It's a 'do care' guide that aims to give people positive lifestyle options.

You can choose to have a caring, loving and supportive relationship with yourself. It's all about finding and connecting to the love within and then allowing it to radiate outwards.

To achieve this, it is important that you have attitudes that make you available for yourself in a positive way; attitudes that ease rather than hinder your progress. It is important to have an emotional agenda that provides a balanced lifestyle and that you make appropriate time for you. It is important to have a mandate that gives you the authority to speak to the world on the same terms as everybody else does, seeing yourself as the equal to anyone and them to you also.

I hope 'It's All About You' will provide you with a new perspective upon yourself; one that is appropriate to your own personal needs. It sets out the grand design, you choose what feels right for you.

ONE – IT'S ALL ABOUT YOU

Our eyes met and locked, gaze steady and unflinching. In a crowded room with little privacy, I desperately wanted to say 'I love you' but I felt too self-conscious. The more I thought about it, the more awkward I felt, as if I was now in the glare of a spotlight and the whole room was looking, but in reality they weren't of course.

Rationality clicked in and I thought to myself how absurd the whole situation was. It went without saying that I love you. I'd always loved you from the first moment and I always would. It should be easy, I mean, I'm a reasonably okay person and sorted emotionally, right? The more I stared into your eyes, the more difficult it became to vocalise my feelings, which surprised me initially and then panicked me when the words still wouldn't come. By now the lump in my throat wasn't helping, nor the tightness in my shoulders as I involuntarily tensed up. My eyes filled with tears and I saw yours did too. God, it was becoming difficult. Perhaps too difficult – should I just get up and go? I can do this I thought; I must do this.

Somehow, I managed to summon every last vestige of courage from my heart and began to mouth the words, "Stephen, I love you". In the handheld mirror, I saw tears well up, as it became shockingly obvious to me that this process was without doubt infinitely more difficult than I could have ever imagined. Uncontrollable sobbing came from the person sitting next door to me, and cautiously, I looked up and surveyed the room. It seemed I wasn't alone, many were discovering unpalatable truths about themselves.

This exercise took place at a healing weekend in London in the mid-nineties. It was a pivotal experience for me, as you can imagine. Previous to this event, I believed I loved myself, and had no obvious examples in my life to make me think otherwise; so why had I encountered such difficulty when asked to declare self-love 'face-to-face' with myself? It seemed to me there had been a gulf between expectation and reality, and it gave me food for thought. It made me consider that perhaps I'd taken it for granted that I loved myself, absolutely and unconditionally, when perhaps I didn't as much as I thought.

This experience set me down a path of self-discovery and personal development, as I sought to get closer to myself. I decided I wanted to make me more available for me, with love and acceptance. Since then, because of my own personal development experiences and from my training and practice as a therapist, I have helped many people turn to themselves in the same way.

The rest of this Book is dedicated to helping you to turn to yourself and showing you how to give yourself what you really need.

Two – Being Your Best Friend And Not Your Worst Enemy

"I wandered lonely as a cloud that floats on high o'er vales and hills, when all at once I saw a crowd, a host of golden daffodils …." (William Wordsworth). A distant voice interjects, becoming louder as you come back to 'reality'. "Come on, stop drifting off into space, that won't help you get anywhere in life. Concentrate on what you're meant to be doing."

Children have a great ability for imagination and letting their minds wander which adults sometimes forget, or even dismiss as being unimportant. Yet openness of mind is crucial for learning and development, because it makes us available for taking on board new ideas and making them our own. As a child, learning about the world is our main preoccupation and we naturally use all of our human gifts in doing so.

Cultivating our knowledge of self happens automatically through our imagination, and this is physically expressed as play. Through 'role play' we learn about relationships and act out the behaviour we learn from people around us; we learn about rules and morals, and about right and wrong. Through these experiences we discover our own individual identities; we discover what makes us happy, and what makes us sad.

As we grow up we also experience criticism and judgement; two very powerful tools used by society to teach us about the realities of our physical world and the laws that govern it.

Experiences such as these transform us from child like beings full of imagination and wonder, into physically practical and purposeful adults. But sometimes criticism and judgment can be overdone, resulting in ultra-competitive environments. The pressure to succeed under such intensity can make us unhappy, or even depressed. This can lead us to reject our true identities until, by adulthood, we have learned another way of being that conforms with what our families and society in general expect of us. This is because deep down we all want to belong.

However, as we mature we also have a greater opportunity to discover the whole of ourselves better. This natural process occurs by an increased understanding of ourselves as we become wiser through experience. Through interacting with life we move through personal milestones and in the process learn more about our identity; we learn how better to relate to our emotions and we adapt our attitudes to suit how we feel about the world.

So where does this self-knowledge come from? The ability to know who we are comes from our consciousness. It is this innate knowledge of self that enables you to be your own guide in the world, to know what is right for you. It enables you to distinguish between what is yours and what is someone else's. It is the little voice inside that tells you to go for it, or to wait and see.

This energy gives you inspiration and it is also your conscience and your intuition. It can be the first flush of excitement felt when greeting somebody or something new in your life, or that instinctive gut feeling that helps you to weigh up a situation to see if it is right for you.

Whatever the event, your inner voice inside needs to be working for you. It needs to be your best friend, not your worst enemy. If it is telling you something that dissuades or even prevents you from expressing your true self, then you need to ask your inner voice if it really loves you. Is it enabling you, or disabling you in life?

We live in a duality of positive and negative, so it follows that we should have both positive and negative self-images. We will sometimes perceive ourselves in a positive way and at other times in a negative way, and this may vary from situation to situation and from day to day.

When we have a positive self-image we will feel generally happy, however if our self-image is predominantly negative we are more likely to feel unhappy. So, in terms of our personal happiness, it logically follows that we need to be able to freely express the knowledge of our positive self-image and encourage its development, while accepting that we will from time to time also exhibit negative characteristics. In other words, if we create and nurture positive attitudes, ideas and emotions about ourselves, and don't dwell too long on the negative, happiness should follow.

It's all about you, so if you treat yourself with love, despite whatever else is going on in the world, you will always have a positive self-relationship. No-one can take that away. As I found out on my healing weekend, thinking positive things about ourselves and actually saying them out loud are two different exercises. Maybe we all have to actually tell ourselves "I love you" to make a proper connection.

I believe in order to get closer to ourselves we need to accept who we are, because you can't really have true love without acceptance; the two are undeniably linked. When you accept yourself you are in effect saying, "It is okay for me to be me and for me to like and love myself."

The following affirmations could be useful in helping you to self-accept, or you could have your own ideas, which is fine; whatever feels appropriate for you. Only you know the words to say and the manner in which to say them to make this process real and meaningful for you. Anyway, here are my ideas. Say them out loud to yourself:

- "I am [*your name*], and I accept who I am"
- "I am me"
- "Its okay for me to be happy"

These affirmations are very powerful statements, because they confer upon us self-acceptance and in turn make us available for self-love. The positive self-image that's generated makes it more difficult for external influences to affect us emotionally and physically, because we have chosen to be us.

If the first step to knowing yourself better is choosing to accept yourself with love, then the second is expressing this knowledge as a best friend would, rather than as a worst enemy.

The saying, "be your best friend, not your worst enemy" is said by people when it appears that somebody is being too hard upon themselves. Essentially 'too hard' means we are rejecting or punishing ourselves, often unfairly and unnecessarily. Therefore, in terms of duality, we are expressing the knowledge of our negative self-image.

In this light, "be your best friend, not your worst enemy" is a command for us to treat ourselves in a positive way, with love and acceptance, rather than negatively with hate and rejection. So, having initiated a positive self-image through our self-acceptance and self loving declarations, how can we build upon it?

In my view, our positive self-image is best supported when we can freely express ourselves with acceptance. But in some situations, we can find it difficult to express ourselves, for fear of being wrong and then criticised; or we are afraid of appearing foolish; or because we are shy, and lack confidence and self-belief. Less now perhaps, but certainly the old Victorian value of children being 'seen but not heard' had legs well into the 20th century and maybe blighted the social development of generations of children.

Having attitudes that encourage you to express yourself is vital to your personal development, because the physical world is the world of expression. It is down to you to make your mark in it; no one else can express for you in the way that you can for yourself.

The physical world allows you to express your mental thoughts, your emotional feelings and your ideas. All those thoughts, ideas, emotions and skills, only become real and are seen to exist when we physically create them. If you don't say it or do it, it stays in your head or heart, going nowhere.

However, what we actually express, and in what manner, is also important. Just remember that everything you physically do or say is a reflection of you. It is your energy; your personality; your self expression. It emanates from, and is created by, you; so symbolically it is you; whether it is making a meal, swinging a golf club, or telling a joke.

If you can welcome your creations into the world and accept them then it follows you are also accepting yourself, while reinforcing the knowledge of your positive self-image. You are being your best friend. Through acceptance we love, and therefore if you can accept your creations you can create self-love.

Likewise, through rejection we hate. So if you act as your worst enemy, putting yourself or your creations down, you reject and therefore hate yourself – subsequently supplementing your negative self-image. Chastising yourself because of a burnt cake, poor golf swing or bad joke only serves to reinforce negatively held views of yourself and your personality.

How can we ensure that we accept everything we do and say though? There are two ways to achieve this:

1) When all is well, we accept though praise and gratitude;

2) When it goes badly, we accept through forgiveness and compassion.

Accepting through praise and gratitude

The simplest way to accept our creations is to praise ourselves for what we have achieved. Recognition is very important and we all like to receive appreciation and thanks for our efforts; so it makes sense that we should praise ourselves as is necessary to confirm our efforts in the world have been worthwhile. "I'm glad I've finished that so well, it was a real challenge."

It is also positive to be grateful for the opportunities we have to express ourselves in this life. For example, we sometimes take our health for granted, but when we 'thank our lucky stars' we are also recognising that our efforts are nothing without the innate energies, talents and skills that aid us to express ourselves in the world.

Accepting through compassion and forgiveness

Accepting ourselves when things go wrong can be harder to do than we realise. When at fault, and it comes down to blaming and shaming, we can be as cruel to ourselves as we can be to other people. Rather than having compassion and forgiveness for our errors and mistakes, our first reaction is often to put ourselves down when we don't really need to ("what a fool I've been"). Else, we blame somebody else ("if he had half a brain he'd be dangerous").

If we can empathise with ourselves when we 'get it wrong' then the burden of blame can be expunged readily through forgiving ourselves. "I gave it my absolute best shot, but it wasn't meant to be" or "it had to be today of all days, well nobody's perfect".

When our performance fails to meet expectations, the shame of our failure can easily be repaired if we have compassion for ourselves. "I can't worry about it, these things happen sometimes" or "oh never mind, there's always another day tomorrow".

Rejecting through criticism

Mostly we are the first to congratulate others on their good news and success, but often we fail to do these things for ourselves.

Perhaps it is because in today's competitive society the 'it could have been better' syndrome is well established. Whatever we say or do, it seems that rather than standing back and acknowledging the worth of our creation, our first thought is always to think of a way in which it could have been improved. The idea being, that if we can finally 'get it right' and attain perfection, we will deserve to receive love, whether from ourselves or from others. Unfortunately, with this attitude all we actually create is self-rejection; and ironically the absolute perfection we desire is destined to remain always out of reach, however hard we try.

Unsurprisingly therefore, it is very common for people in our culture, where the perfect body and self-image is prized, to subconsciously or knowingly reject themselves because they feel inadequate, undeserving or worse still, failures. In a superficial way, we tell ourselves we cannot be happy because we are too fat, or too thin, or ugly, unsuccessful, stupid, poor etc. etc., even if this is not true in reality. If we are overly self-critical and rarely praise ourselves, we are automatically downgrading our achievements, and will judge everything we do, however good it may be, as a failure. It is hard to imagine how we can be happy under such conditions.

Chapter Summary

To have compassion and forgiveness for ourselves is not about 'letting yourself off the hook', 'looking for excuses' or 'countenancing failure'; it is about keeping your response to situations positive and preserving your positive self-image through acceptance. It's about being your best friend and not your worst enemy. Blaming and shaming just serves to confirm the poor opinion we have of ourselves and strengthens our negative self-image through rejection of self.

So be kind to you. You have the option to create self-love if you want to. You can choose to express yourself and accept your creations through praise, graditude, forgiveness and compassion. 'Express and accept' could be your new buzzword if you wish. Next time you find yourself being over critical and putting yourself down, try to catch and stop yourself doing it, revise your attitudes and thinking, and instead accept what you've done in a positive way. Oh, and don't forget to give yourself a pat on the back when things are going well.

I hope you've seen how important is it to realise and understand what happens to us when we express ourselves and subsequently how useful it is to build those perceptions into our lives in a helpful and positive way. Even if others criticise you, you mustn't do it to yourself. Even if others judge you, you mustn't do it to yourself. From today forgive and have compassion for yourself. From today, feel and be responsible for your own happiness.

Just remember, everything you express into this reality is a reflection of you, so you can't afford to allow yourself to criticise or reject your self-image. Instead, welcome yourself into your life and throw out a red carpet for you. You are a VIP in your world.

From this point on in your life, be your best friend and not your worst enemy.

Three – All You Need Is A Little Give And Take?

What is the driving force that determines why you behave in the way you do? You are. You have the power to choose how you express yourself. You will act in some situations to try to get what you want, and in other situations you may want to give way to what others want.

But why? The motivation that governs our behaviour in relationships is our need to create self esteem; and this traditionally works in two different ways:

- Firstly, you can obtain self-esteem through giving to others. By supporting other people, and showing willingness, you can demonstrate your worth and gain their liking.

- Secondly, you can gain self-esteem through taking. By guiding others, and showing leadership, you can prove yourself to them and gain their respect.

Givers are people who like to stand back and see what everybody else is proposing first. Their natural inclination is to follow others' suggestions above their own, because they see their primary role as supporting the needs of others. This means the Giver will always seek to give responsibility in a relationship by ceding it to you, because through their giving they obtain a sense of self-esteem. Therefore Givers are generally uncompetitive people who gain pleasure from helping others.

Takers are people who like to lead from the front and take charge of situations. The Taker will assess a situation and provide an opinion that they will try to convince others to follow, because they see their main role in life as guiding the needs of others. The Taker will readily assume responsibility in a relationship because it gives them the opportunity to prove themselves. Takers are mainly competitive people, who derive excitement from organising and controlling situations on behalf of others.

For every person who stands back there will be one who leads, and so for every Giver there is a Taker. Further, every one of us can be a Giver in some situations and a Taker in others.

Whether you're a Giver or a Taker you are relying on the relationship with another person to create, or reinforce, your self-esteem. While the relationship is balanced, with one giving and one taking, both parties will indeed feel good about themselves. But what happens if one of them gets tired of the situation? What if the Giver decides its time to take something for themselves, or the Taker rejects what the Giver offers?

For instance, people can become ill with chronic long-term physical and/or emotional illnesses, or they may discover that their partner is having an affair. In these circumstances, they can find it difficult to support their lifestyle, either because of a lack of energy and enthusiasm or from the heartbreak they suffer, and this further compounds their feelings of unhappiness. The Giver feels they cannot cope any longer, while the Taker thinks they are a failure.

At this point the Giver will usually try to give more and more in an attempt to feel worthy, and the Taker will usually try to take more and more in an attempt to prove them self. However this just exacerbates the problem. Rather than turning to others to prop up their self-esteem, they could to turn to themselves for the answers they need.

Turning to yourself and becoming an Awarer

When you say, "turn to yourself" to a Giver, they think this means they have to be selfish and can't bear the thought of taking. When you say, "turn to yourself" to a Taker, they think they have to be selfless and give up everything they have accumulated and they can't bear the loss of face.

It is not a case of asking the Giver to be 'self-ish' or the taker to be 'self-less', but instead both to be self-aware.

Being self-aware means you love yourself for who you are, not because of what you give or take through interacting with other people. By expressing and accepting your creations, you can build your esteem through self-love.

Awarers choose to express their love into their relationships, rather than wholly relying on their relationships to provide them with love and identity. If both partners love themselves first, then they are more able to accept and love each other.

In this case, love becomes a mutual consensus, arrived at through a joint motivation to be accepted. Consequently, Awarers seek parity in their relationships to achieve their goals. By desiring fairness and equality, a point of equilibrium is reached in their relationships, whereby both parties feel equally loved. They express themselves on the basis, "I love you as much as I love myself". This ethic becomes the basis upon which their understanding of love and acceptance is built.

This means they choose not to put their self-interest above or below other people's, but in line with them. Awarers will not choose for you, or let others choose for them, but will agree on a mutually beneficial choice together.

For example, imagine you are in a car showroom. You're looking for a little economical model for taking the kids to school and running down to the shops, and you explain this to the salesman. However what you don't know is that he's been told they need to shift more of the top of the range 'XT Turbo Sport', and he gets double commission for each one of these he sells.

The Taker salesman would clearly try his absolute hardest to get you to buy the 'XT Turbo Sport', coming up with a host of reasons why you would need a supercharged 16 cylinder engine, capable of 0-60 in 4.5 seconds to get Charlie to his nursery in the next village. The Giver salesman would still try to sell you the 'XT Turbo Sport', detailing how it could suit your needs, but would offer you a large discount to tempt you, thus eating significantly into his commission.

However, the Awarer salesman wouldn't try to push any particular model onto you. He would ask what your requirements were, listen to your reply, give you all the relevant facts about each model, and leave you to decide what was best for you. Result, you get the car you need, he gets a sale with a fair commission.

Approaching life in this way means you take responsibility for your own happiness. This is not being selfish, because you are not taking from others and it is not selfless, because you are not giving to others.

When you know and love yourself, the perspective it provides can help you in your relationships with other people. It is easier to forgive others and have compassion for them, if your own sense of self is better developed. It's easier to see the boundaries in your relationships, and what's your 'stuff' and what's theirs. It becomes easier not to take things said or done by other people so personally. If they fail to meet you half way or are unkind, as an Awarer you can see clearly that it's just their own self-rejection talking. It's nothing to do with you really and it isn't your fault.

It means that when others criticise you, as a Taker does to gain control, or refuse to accept your praise, as a Giver does to appear worthy, you can understand their behaviour better – 'it's their stuff.' This understanding allows Awarers to accept other people, through forgiving or having compassion for the other person (or indeed themselves) as is appropriate. As we saw earlier, practising forgiveness and compassion means that acceptance can still be created when things go wrong; unlike blaming and shaming, which just creates rejection.

Why is it that turning to ourselves can be so difficult? Often it is our attitudes that stop us; making us feel guilty or a failure. The next chapter looks at attitudes and the important part they play in our lives.

FOUR – IT'S ALL ABOUT ATTITUDES

Everybody is different and so is their understanding of themselves and the world. Our view upon life is shaped initially in childhood where we learn attitudes from others and society. These attitudes continue to influence us as adults, until we arrive at our own 'take' on the world. However, we may have acquired attitudes as children that don't necessarily reflect how we now perceive ourselves, and the world to be. For instance you may have been told you were a failure academically at school, but found at work you had a dynamic personality that gained you friends and managerial promotion.

The intention of this chapter is to help you develop your understanding of how attitudes are formed, how they affect us and how we 'acquire' attitudes from others that influence our behaviour and our lives.

If you feel that your physical environment denies you free expression, then the knowledge of your identity will be limited to those conditions. In other words, you will only be able to express what is allowable rather than what you really think and feel.

Are you easily able to be you?

This may seem a rather strange question, but it is not always easy for us to express our true selves. Imagine you were surrounded by a crowd of people that you respected and considered to be very important, maybe a little in awe of, and they all insisted that brown was the most awful colour imaginable, and the only colour to be seen in this year was purple; how easy would you find it to take off your coat and show them your chocolate brown suit, beige shirt and tan coloured tie?

This may seem a rather trivial example, but what if you were to substitute the colours in the above example with the 'peer pressure'? What if everyone around you is working two hours unpaid overtime every day, and is constantly bitching about 'Mary in accounts' who goes home at 5pm on the dot? Come 5.00 you just want to go home to spend some quality time with your family, but could you leave off then; or would you say you loved your job and stay until 7.00?

This sort of situation is okay if it only happens occasionally, and you are able to freely express yourself most of the time; but if you suppress your true thoughts and feelings too often and for too long this can lead to unhappiness and despair. Eventually you will reach a point where you can't take it any more; 'the final straw that broke the camel's back' and you will inevitably rebel. This can be a real shock, not only to yourself, but to those around you who had been under the impression that you were happy to go along with them.

The limits that we perceive in our physical world occur through the relationships we have with our parents, children, relations, friends, school and work. As we grow up the people close to us attempt to mould us into the 'perfect' person, by teaching us patterns of behaviour that are socially acceptable and 'in our best interests'. This 'social conditioning' continues, albeit usually in a more subtle way, as we enter adulthood, go out to work and throughout the rest of our lives.

Social conditioning is constantly evolving, because it mirrors what is happening in our society. Every century has been different to the one before it in the history of humankind. What society deems is acceptable behaviour varies from year to year and decade to decade.

Our knowledge of past decades is enhanced by 'retro' shows on television, which discuss fashions and attitudes from a particular decade and enable us to identify with the stereotypes they create. For instance, in the stereotypical view of the 60s everyone wore flowers in their hair and believed in peace and love; but in the 80s they wore shoulder pads, had 'big hair' and believed in big business and making money.

Within this evolutionary process, we learn and adapt to changing attitudes in order to reflect and maintain our own social position. We learn to modify our behaviour to suit the social occasion. Consequently, we are constantly projecting out an image of ourselves that tells people who we are in any given situation and which is acceptable to ourselves and to others.

Also, our behaviour is usually different at work to when we are with family and friends. Neither image is necessarily a reflection of our true selves however; sometimes we choose to project an image of what others expect us to be in order to please and retain an accord with them, rather than express how we really feel. So sometimes we compromise ourselves to fit in with the requirements of the particular situation; or the reverse could be true, and we may try to persuade other people to fit in with us. Whichever is true, we are dependant upon our relationship with another person, or a social group, to give us the knowledge of who we are.

The gift of our physical reality is that it enables us to express ourselves. Speech helps us to relate our personality to other people, and vice versa. However, if you cede the right to express yourself to somebody else, then they will be communicating to the world on your behalf.

For example, when we vote for a particular politician we are in effect ceding to them our right to make decisions about our community. We may not get the politician we voted for, and we may not always agree with what they say or do, but we accept it as they were freely elected by the majority. In totalitarian or 'big brother' states, however, the citizen is encouraged to toe the party line, at least in public, and express the official opinion – rather than their own. Under these conditions, individual freedom of expression is suppressed.

This national scenario can also occur in our personal relationships. Can you think of instances where other people have dominated you rather like a dictator would? Ignoring your opinions, speaking on your behalf and denying you the right to express yourself in the way you'd like? Or indeed do you sometimes find yourself acting like the dictator? Whichever role you may play, ask yourself does it make you feel truly happy? Or do you really feel disappointed or ashamed or angry with yourself?

As we discussed in Chapter 2, we need to learn to love and accept ourselves if we are to cultivate a positive self-image, and it is important that our attitudes reflect this mandate.

What is an attitude?

An attitude is a combination of stored emotional and mental intent. It is a stored experience or memory that we recall when faced with a similar situation to help us to know how to behave. In order to survive and protect ourselves, we learn to sum up situations very quickly. For example, "is there a threat to me here?"; "do I understand enough about this by myself or, if not, who should I ask for help?" etc. etc.

The following example shows the processes involved in constructing an attitude and also how it is subsequently reinforced through use.

Ever since I can remember, I have liked the colour blue. When I choose to wear this colour my identity is therefore reflected in it, because it is worn for me. I know it suits me and therefore I like to wear it. This gives me pleasurable feelings and in doing so emotionally I see this colour as my favourite. Mentally I have rationalised this experience, and through analysis and experience I am able to decide when to wear blue, in what combination with other colours and what the level of influence it should have in my life. For example, if I need to buy a new car does it need to be blue? This attitude is 'made real' and reinforced every time I choose to express it in the physical world, such as choosing to paint my kitchen walls with blue paint. If somebody asks me my favourite colour, it's unlikely I will debate this question from scratch with myself, because I already know what my attitude is and what my response will be; blue!

Reflect for a minute upon your own attitudes and your own personal likes and dislikes. They are of you, reflecting how you feel about yourself and revealing your personal view of the world.

Do you have attitudes that say, "I love who I am" and "I can do this"? Or, do you have attitudes that say, "I dislike who I am" and "There's just no way I can do this"? Whatever your attitudes may be, they all have one thing in common with each other; they are all of the past until you draw upon them in the present.

Past experiences play a large part in our judgement of present situations, in how we will deal with them and how we communicate what we have done to others. For example, if you've already failed five driving tests your expectation of passing the sixth will probably not be very high. Your attitude may well be "I'll never manage to pass that test". Conversely, if you passed your driving test on the first attempt you will probably feel pretty confident about taking the test to get your Heavy Goods Vehicle license. Your attitude will probably be "It's only an overgrown car! I can drive it with no problem."

You can see our attitudes can promote or demote us; build us up, or deflate us; make us believe we can tackle anything, or make us doubt ourselves. So it is important that we try to keep them in perspective.

We should view past memories and the attitudes they produce purely as a way to assist us and guide us to safely express ourselves, and never as a vehicle for self-rejection. So if you make a mistake, remember it's not the end of the world; whatever the end result is, it is in your power to forgive and have compassion for yourself; and the next time you are in the same situation your attitude will hopefully guide you to act in a different way and not repeat the same mistake.

If we have attitudes that run counter to their intended and positive use then surely we owe it to ourselves to send them packing? But keeping strong in the face of persuasion or temptation can be difficult; and if we have attitudes that are working to prevent us expressing ourselves, for fear of failure, appearing ridiculous, unworthy or 'un-cool,' we could be missing opportunities to represent ourselves in the world.

If you have trouble expressing what you really feel inside, or you feel inappropriate negative emotions in situations, then you have attitudes that are working against you. These attitudes have almost certainly been put there by others and you have come to accept them as your own. You have acquired attitudes.

Acquired attitudes

When we accept the attitude of another above our own, then we acquire their attitude. This can have a positive or negative affect upon us, depending upon the role model we chose.

You know the story, boy meets girl, and the stronger personality dominates the other. The weaker personality changes their life, stops seeing their friends, rebels against their family, or even cuts them out of their lives altogether; whatever they need to do to make the other person 'happy'. This could be because of a lack of self-confidence, or because they are totally besotted with the new person, or any number of other reasons. But, whatever it is, they are clearly influenced enough to express attitudes other than their own. Sometimes the change is so dramatic; it's as if you suddenly don't know them any longer. In effect, you lose them to their dominant partner, or that's how it seems.

Equally, you hear the tale of somebody who is constantly in trouble meeting a person who changes their life in a positive way by lifting them out of their destructive patterns. The former wild child is tamed, settles down and goes on to have a happy and contented family life.

Generally though, the effects of acquired attitudes on our personalities are much less obvious. We see something in another person's behaviour or personality that we like and resolve to try to be more like them. Maybe you view yourself as shy and timid, and want to be more like someone you see as confident and outgoing; or maybe you think you have a tendency to be selfish, and want to be more like the considerate person who gave up their seat for you on the bus. If we can acquire attitudes that we consider to be positive we will enhance our positive image of ourselves, thus topping up our self-esteem and leading us to a greater acceptance of ourselves.

As children it is important for our own safety and growth to listen and learn from the caring adults around us, but we can also acquire some much less helpful attitudes during our formative years. In the vast majority of cases parents have their child's best interests at heart. They want them to have all the things that they felt they never had, and be the happiest person that they can be; however their methods can quite often lead to the opposite result.

When a child is born it has no acquired attitudes; it is a truly pure and innocent person, a blank canvas, wanting nothing more than to love and be loved. But then at 1 year old he starts to walk and talk and explore the world; he picks up his mother's empty coffee mug and drops it; or he runs down the garden and out onto the road; or he tries to climb over the stair gate. In each instance his parents are concerned for his safety; but do they express this by hugging him and saying he shouldn't do it because he will hurt himself? Or do they just tell him off for being 'naughty'. The first option teaches him the attitude that he needs to exercise caution in some situations to avoid injuring himself; and the second teaches him that he is naughty and "can't do anything right".

Or what about the six year old who brings home a painting she did at school that day? Does her father praise her creation and stick it straight up on the wall, thus helping to reinforce her positive self-image; or does he point out that the sky should really be blue, not pink, and he has never seen purple grass before? Although intended to help her to do a better painting next time, if he chooses this second reaction and acts in a similar way in other situations it will just instil in his daughter the attitude that her creations are never good enough.

Negative attitudes acquired in our childhood are the hardest ones to come to terms with, because they have been a part of us for so long. But if we want to move on and extricate ourselves from their influence we must come to terms with them; and also try to forgive the person we acquired them from.

You are the only person that can decide if an attitude is right for you, and if it is truly working in your best interests. You may already be aware of negative attitudes that you have acquired, but it can be difficult to challenge the power of them. Knowing you have an attitude that is not working for you is one thing, but finding the strength inside to let it go, or even accepting that it has to go, is another game altogether. Be assured, however, the knowledge, power and strength to do this is accessible to all of us. Its worth remembering, there are no limits, only those we seek to self-impose.

Be your own judge. Life is about cause and effect. We express ourselves and get a reaction, whether from ourselves or from those around us. You have the right to choose how you feel about yourself and how you want to lead your life. Often, we have attitudes that prevent us from taking control of our lives in a positive way. How you feel after expressing yourself will tell you if you have acquired negative attitudes.

Everybody wants to love and feel good about themselves. But sometimes you may feel an inappropriate response from expressing yourself, such as feeling guilty for spending a little time on watching your favourite movie; or angry that you ate a piece of chocolate when you're supposed to be on a diet.

Assuming that you're not watching the movie when you should be picking up your five year old from school, is there really any harm in allowing yourself a couple of hours 'me time' occasionally? And is eating a little piece of chocolate really going to make you gain 2 pounds in weight? Of course not. Clearly then these attitudes are not working in your best interest, so it follows that you must have acquired them from someone else and made them your own. Maybe you remember your father saying "you won't have time to sit around watching movies when you get older, you'll have too many other things to do", or your mother saying "don't eat too many sweets – they'll make you fat"?

At this point, listen to yourself and do what feels right for you. Is it expressing an attitude that helps you to love and accept yourself ("I love that film, now I feel ready to get on with my chores" or "Mmm that chocolate was good – now back to the salads"), or an attitude that helps you to hate and reject yourself? It should be an easy choice, but often its not, because we all have experience of feeling terrible about ourselves when we shouldn't really, but for some reason it seems sometimes we just can't help it. This is the power of acquired attitudes. But what we can acquire, we can let go. As adults, we can choose to write or rewrite our own life scripts. Sure, honour those examples from earlier times that you wish to keep, but it is also okay to jettison those attitudes and mindsets that now harm or hinder your progress.

So the next time you are doing something you enjoy, but then start to feel bad about it for no reason, reject this feeling and concentrate on self-acceptance; telling yourself its okay for you to be happy. If you can accept what you create you are choosing to allow a positive feel-good to stay with you, helping to trigger feelings of happiness and wellbeing.

We all have attitudes that are preventing us from connecting to ourselves in the way we would like, but it is vital for your happiness and sense of self-worth to foster attitudes that enable you to create love and acceptance.

Five - Your Agenda For Living

The main bar to achieving a balanced and happy lifestyle is not a lack of time in which to do things, it is the way we treat ourselves. It is your life and the way you are leading it that is the most important thing, not necessarily the amount of time you have to spend.

The Agenda for Living is a lifestyle model. It aims to show you how you can prioritise your 'style of life' to maximise your potential to create love and acceptance. Essentially, it is an Awarer agenda; this means remembering to be your best friend, through expressing and accepting yourself; rather than being your worst enemy, expressing and rejecting.

The Agenda is therefore an emotional and not a time model, and the emotion it is most concerned with is love. It orders your personal obligations into a hierarchy that reflects your ability to create love; but of course you will still determine the length of time you personally spend on each.

You have a whole host of duties, commitments, obligations and agreements with a variety of people and institutions, which you must perform in your daily life. Generally these will usually be to yourself, your children, parents, siblings, other relatives, friends and work. Briefly, list these examples for yourself in the order you deem of most importance.

You should have a list that begins with you. Remember, it is the quality of your relationship with yourself that determines how happy and contented you feel in your life. So if you have placed yourself at the bottom of your list, and are looking horror struck at it, doubting how or why you should ever climb further up it, then your lifestyle and attitudes are almost certainly working against you. If you've placed everything else in your life before yourself then it must follow that you're supporting the emotional interests of others before your own.

Positive self-esteem comes from meeting your own emotional needs first. You can't be truly happy if your life doesn't allow you to love and feel good about you. So, if you can keep to your duty to accept and love yourself, you will find yourself at the top of your list.

Additionally, if you love yourself, you will also seek to create equality in your relationships with other people; you neither take from them, nor let them take advantage of you. Therefore the awareness that self-love brings eventually benefits everybody. It can instigate a positive change from within, which transmutes externally and improves the quality of all your relationships, creating parity and a spirit of fairness in them.

Let's look more closely at the Agenda.

The Agenda for Living

DUTIES	yourself; children
RESPONSIBILITIES	partner; adult children; parents; parents-in-law; brothers and sisters; other relatives; close friends
COMMITMENTS	work
AGREEMENTS	friends

The above table shows where our emotional priorities should lie in order to maximise our potential to create love. Problems can occur when we mismatch the order of our obligations we have to other people and institutions. For example, if we make our work a duty, in terms of its importance in our lives, we are likely to be placing it above our personal needs and possibly our families; and we are gaining esteem from our professional success, rather than from our love relationships.

Or, if we make the relationship with our partner a duty, then we've probably placed them 'on a pedestal,' and are relying on them to make us feel loved. However, if this is not reciprocated we can be making ourselves available for them to take advantage of us. This doesn't just have to apply to our relationship with our partner, it could also be parents, children or any other person we deem to be more important than ourselves. Such as the adoring Mother who allows her adult son, who still lives at home, to treat her house like a hotel. Or the guilty father, who spends money on his teenage daughter and spoils her, because he spends too much time at work.

Our obligations, and how they should be ordered and why, is explained in greater detail below.

Duties

DUTY: A moral or legal obligation. The binding force of what is right. What is required of one.

A duty is the act of unconditionally giving/loving. We choose to make ourselves available in a specific role, without any strings attached.

In society, some people feel 'duty bound' to perform a task which is necessary for the greater whole, or to take on the burdens of others. These include politicians, health workers, policeman, members of the armed forces, and others in public service. The Queen is the embodiment of duty in the way she performs her role, an example to those who in turn perform duties in her name.

We are all familiar with the above examples of duty, but these are all external to ourselves. At a personal level, your duty is to love and protect yourself. To love through the right of self-expression and self-acceptance; and to protect through safeguarding your identity from the unwanted attentions of others.

The Agenda for Living puts this duty at the very top of the list, because having a quality relationship with yourself is paramount in ensuring that all the other relationships in your life work with you. It also acknowledges that to truly love another, you need to know and love your self first. If you don't love your self, then you are reliant upon feeling love through another person.

The Agenda for Living also accepts that we have an equal duty to our underage children as we have to ourselves. Until they are old enough to know themselves and take responsibility for their own lives, it is natural for us to perform this duty on their behalf. We have a duty to give our young children love, protection, guidance and encouragement in an environment that supports their growing identity and enables them to have faith and belief in themselves. How can we properly fulfil this duty if we neglect ourselves and fail to build these characteristics in us?

After all, children identify strongly with their parents, learning from examples set by them. Therefore they can only be a reflection of you. All their imperfections are yours also.

Responsibilities

RESPONSIBILITY: The state or fact of being responsible; the ability to act independently and take decisions; the person or thing for which one is responsible.

A responsibility is a conditional act. In a physical sense you acquire an interest for which you are responsible. For example, if you have invested money into a limited liability business and in return you have sought financial gain, then physically you are responsible up to the limit of your investment. Your responsibility is the fact you have given the money, but it is conditional upon a return of profit. In other words, you have given and you want something back.

We can also translate this at a relationship level, where each party holds a stake in it and seeks to profit from their participation.

My definition of responsibility is to say that the level of our interest in any relationship should be limited to achieving equity with other interested parties. We should neither seek loss nor gain, allowing each to have an equal share. This creates a trusting environment that enables each party to express their own identity in the relationship in a safe and mutually beneficial way through cooperation.

In the Agenda for Living you have a duty to express and accept yourself, while you have a responsibility towards others that enables them to do the same. In essence, this means your responsibility towards others is to contribute in creating an environment whereby they can also express and accept themselves. This means as one party expresses themselves, the other is responsible for accepting them, and vice versa. In this way they act like a mirror, because through accepting you, your identity is reflected and revealed back as a creation of love. They also get to see your reflection and share in the knowledge of this experience.

When you enter into a serious relationship, whether formally through marriage or informally through common law; from that point on your relationships with other family members are changed. Your partner becomes your most important responsibility, above all other family members (except of course underage children, who you still have a duty to nurture). Conflicts can arise during this period, as all parties need to accept the change.

As we grow up and become adults we have an opportunity to find ourselves. We may choose to live by the example shown by our parents and from learned experience in society, from our schooling for example; or we may choose to find our own values. Whichever is true, the transition into adulthood is a time of change. As young adults we need to be able to take responsibility for our own lives, and parents need to be able to give it. Certainly, we should be thankful and respectful of our parents' efforts in bringing us up, but at some point we have to find our own way. As in any relay race, achieving a trouble free pass of the baton can be difficult; and passing responsibility can be near impossible if there is no meeting of minds - if the young adult doesn't want to take it or if the parent doesn't want to give it.

To show the distinction between old and new, we usually hold a party to mark the coming of age in our society; for example, at eighteen years old you become legally responsible. This ritual signifies to everyone else the change in the status. It is a major change in the parents' life, because their relationship to their child drops from a duty to a responsibility. It is also a major change for the young adult, who has taken over the duty to love and protect their own self and should not rely on their parents for their identity. They also now have a responsibility to their parents.

This doesn't mean you stop loving your children or parents now, it just means the young adult has a duty to run their own life. The parents' and young adults' responsibility to each other means they should always be available, when invited, to offer love and support in times of need and to expect the same in return. This is true of all your relationships with parents, brothers and sisters and other relations, as you build your own family. Yes, they do move down in terms of importance on your Agenda for Living, but it doesn't mean you stop loving them.

All this serves to demonstrate how family ties are extremely important and good relationships between family members help us to express the emotional love we feel for them and ourselves.

Commitments

COMMITMENT: An engagement or obligation that restricts freedom of action; the process or instance of committing oneself; a pledge or undertaking.

A commitment is where we give a conditional undertaking to perform a specified role, in return for something that we are content to accept. The contract of employment is one such a commitment. Your job description is a legally binding contract, asking you to undertake specified tasks for which you are remunerated with a monetary payment or other benefits. At a purely physical level, money and status are the only tangible elements that come out of the job you do. As long as you feel you have performed to the terms of the contract, you will demand payment for your efforts. You get out what you put in and the employer acknowledges the energy you have expended when they pay you. The contract is performed and settled, both parties are satisfied.

At an emotional level, the fact we are giving is acknowledged and returned when the employer appreciates our efforts. Energy is transferred like this: you give; the employer receives; they appreciate you and so it is returned back to you. They are happy that you have performed to the contract and give back by thanking you. You take esteem by feeling proud, from having proved your talents and skills in successfully completing your specified tasks. Both parties are contented within this relationship and the energy between the two is balanced and grounded. This is an explanation of job satisfaction. You feel you have done the job well and you take confirmation of this by their thanks and recognition of your abilities.

As the payment is material however, the nature of the work relationship tends to be more formal than with family members. In the first instance, all that is required is for the employee to work and the employer to pay. We have seen how this transaction affects a physical transfer of energy, but we only become satisfied emotionally through job satisfaction. It is for this reason that a job is only a commitment. Family and other relationships come above that, because we have an opportunity to express love and receive it back at a deeper level than we do through our jobs.

Agreements

AGREEMENTS: The holding of the same opinion; Mutual understanding; an arrangement between parties as to a course of action; Harmony.

An agreement is a meeting of minds between different parties. From this mutual understanding a relationship can begin. This best defines the workings of a friendship.

Friends are people you have a relationship with because you initially have a common interest or attraction. You can express yourself with them in a way that makes you feel good. Friendships and their nature vary from person to person and situation to situation. They can last for life or be just fleeting, but whichever is true at their basis is a mutual agreement to share your expression with another human being.

It is just this capacity to share which makes some people love their friends, for while they are with them they can truly be themselves and vice-versa. This is even truer if they find their family structure is heavily formalised, where its members inter-relate by status e.g. the stereotypical dutiful son/daughter relationship with their father/mother; where they are required to perform a specified role, rather than be themselves.

It may be that outside of your immediate household most of the people you love are your friends. In some cases a friend may assume a greater importance in our lives above that of other family members. This is especially true of siblings when their lives take them in different directions and so our friends can become surrogate family. If both friends value each other at this level, then of course the nature of their relationship changes from an agreement to a responsibility.

Chapter Summary

You have learned that if you can try to approach everything you do as an Awarer, (i.e. giving yourself what you need, but not at the expense of anyone else; and helping others, but not at your own expense) this will lead you to accept and subsequently learn to love yourself for who you are. But incorporating this into your life through implementing your own Agenda for Living can be quite difficult, especially if you've been taught to always put yourself last.

If you're finding it hard to commit emotionally yourself, or are unhappy with yourself, then sometimes it's necessary to devote extra physical time to you in order to create a positive self-image

Our modern lifestyles seem to demand we need more energy than we can possibly ever have to fulfil our obligations. This statement translates in our lives as doing more than we can cope with, which can lead to us feeling stressed or 'burnt out.' The next Chapter sees how worthwhile it is to create extra time in our lives if we need to.

Six – 'Batten Down The Hatches And Make Yourself Available For You'

"Stephen, what can I do to help me relax?" I motioned my client onto the couch, before pausing and thinking? "Have you got any hobbies, I asked?" "Well no, not really. I find my work is my hobby, because I enjoy it so much."

It was obvious to me that this person had little time to spend on himself. I thought to myself that trying to push square-pegged work into a round-holed hobby would never make a perfect match. Better if he could separate them and allow each to provide a different experience, through enjoying being at work and by relaxing through a hobby. Then, I concluded, he would be playing to his strengths. I still didn't know if it was through choice or a need that he worked such long hours, but at least he was happy in his job.

And this is the point here; how much time do we have just for us to express ourselves? Probably, our greatest lifestyle conflict concerns our work/life balance. Usually, this means we are working too long and not having enough quality time with our families and friends.

In our culture, there is a strongly developed work ethic. The UK has the longest working hours on average in Europe. Some people need to work long hours to provide money for their families just to survive; while others do it to improve their standard of living; and some choose to do it just because it gives them a buzz and makes them feel good. If you can afford to though, or your job will let you, it makes good sense to plan for leisure time because doing activities away from work will give you a different connection to you.

The standards by which we measure success are set by society, and for many people the challenge that modern life presents us with now is the pressure to be competitive The subsequent ability to respond is our stress. At work, more is expected of us and in less time and quite often there is just minimal support. Subsequently, life becomes more survivalist and when this happens we tend to respond in a more physical and less emotional way. You do what you have to do in order to get by.

There is also less room for sentiment in a 'them or me' environment and so our personalities become shaped by the desire to win at all costs; we are terrified to be seen as a 'loser' - where we could get passed over for promotion, or worse still we believe we could become demoted or made redundant. Without income, our lifestyles and material gains diminish and so does our social status and feelings of self-worth. Ultimately, under these conditions we get esteem and satisfaction from feeling that we are coping and by proving that we are meeting our goals – work doesn't have to be fun we tell ourselves.

If you are caught up in this frame of mind, or maybe you know people who are, you will probably view a commitment to make more time available for yourself as either an admission of failure, if you are a Taker, or of being unworthy, if you are a Giver. In the choppy seas of today's lifestyles, it takes a determined effort to change course and this is why the image of battening down the hatches of a ship is used to illustrate this point. There's the challenge, but how to meet it and make time for you?

Battening Down the Hatches.

Like most other things in life, if you want to create a positive self-image, you will need to devote the necessary time and commitment to achieving it. 'Battening down the hatches' symbolically reflects the point when you turn to yourself with this purpose in mind. This commitment could manifest as a simple change in attitudes and behaviour towards yourself and others; or if you are stressed and unhappy it could involve large scale changes, re-jigging your schedule to devote extra time to yourself, in order to feel good about you again.

As a therapist, I tell my clients 'perspective is everything'. Especially when we are stressed and unhappy our take on the world can seem bleak and even desperate, and once you get stuck in this hole it can be difficult for you to see the woods for the trees. Instead of coping with challenges, you feel like you're sinking, completely overwhelmed or lost for ideas; in other words, you lose perspective. Stress, the modern day curse, is responsible for more sick days taken from work than anything else, even back-pain.

Stress in itself isn't necessarily a bad thing; it is when it turns negative that it becomes a problem. Negative stress is a perceived failure by people to meet an agreed performance level or fulfil their obligations. This means they are effectively giving free rein to negative self expression and judgement. Sometimes this is the root cause of their stress, or else it may subsequently serve to compound it. This results in physical, mental and emotional side effects, such as unhappiness, poor sleep, anxiety etc.

The 'agreed performance level' from the paragraph above can often be self-imposed, and not necessarily what others around you or your employer expects. I often see cases where people expect too much of themselves and set unrealistic performance targets which they struggle to meet. Of course if you have unrealistic goals, whether they are self-imposed or set for you by your employer, teacher, parent or partner, there is a high probability that you will fail; and if this happens it will do nothing for your positive self-image.

Another cause of negative stress is people's perceived failure to 'fulfil their obligations'. People who spread themselves too thin; doing this that and the other for every other Tom, Dick and Harry, while crucially ignoring their own needs. They are way too busy to properly have quality time with anybody, especially themselves. They chase here there and everywhere, no wonder they are stressed – its making me feel anxious just writing about it!

Work hard, play hard lifestyles can be very exciting and rewarding, and if people have the energy then this is great. Modern day 'full on' lifestyles, rely on driving the nervous system to the limit; but burning the candle at both ends and pushing yourself too hard for too long inevitably leads to stress and exhaustion. If left unchecked it can even lead to a complete nervous breakdown, as you lose your sense of identity to your hectic lifestyle; in effect you become your job, your family, your duties and commitments.

If in crisis, my simple advice to my clients is 'get back to you. Create a safe knowledge of you based on self acceptance and love, through doing something that you enjoy doing. It can be anything; as long as it creates time for you it will help boost your self-esteem and make you feel good about yourself again. When this happens, you will have regained a positive perspective, and this knowledge will help you to see what you need to do to sort out the problem areas of your life.' It is very important that we make time for ourselves, however we are feeling, as I believe our leisure time gives us the best opportunity to constructively improve our self-image.

Jobs, tasks, chores etc. deliver just what they mean. They are absolutely necessary to ensure the proper functioning of the world, but our esteem comes from giving, and then taking the satisfaction that comes from completing our tasks.

But if you can also reserve some time for expressing your energy solely for yourself, in a way that makes you happy, you will create a stronger connection to you. A bad day at work doesn't need to be such a drag if you can regain a positive experience of yourself through a hobby when you get home. Consequently, the fast track to knowing and loving yourself and improving your self-relationship is through pastimes, hobbies and interests. They deliver to you what they say.

When we are into something we enjoy, it can become so engrossing that we lose track of time. Time passes; hence the meaning of the word pastimes. The feel good factor created through pastimes and hobbies stays with us, helping us to readily cement into place the knowledge of who we are and reinforcing our positive self-image. It really is that simple, but it's also so difficult, because in our busy lives it is often hard to find the time in which to do these things.

If we do not find any time for us during the week, and anyway are always critical of what we are doing, then it is hard to imagine how we can be happy. In fact we are likely to be unhappy, and in resignation will probably put it down to the modern pace of life with its ever increasing pressures and stress.

The easiest way to connect to yourself is physically. During exercise it's your muscles that work, your heart that pumps and your lungs that breathe. It's no one else's, not your bosses, not your partners, not your parents. Physical interests can give you an immediate connection to yourself purely because it is your body that is working. Not only can it make you feel fitter, but exercise also enables the body to release hormones that ease stress and worries. Anyone who does it regularly will tell you that going for a walk can ease worries. Seemingly the physical exercise can provide a fresh perspective by clearing our heads of unwanted thoughts, providing an answer and/or magically making the worry irrelevant.

As well as taking our minds away from stress, pastimes and hobbies can also help to improve our mental processes and develop concentration, such as by doing crosswords, reading books, woodworking, cross-stitch etc. When reading, we are using mental processes to create images in our head of the story, through our imagination. Eventually we can feel like we are in the story, even as one of the characters. By this time our emotions are responding to the situations encountered in the plot, providing a riveting and wonderful enjoyment. Likewise, how often do you get so engrossed in a film, that when a loud noise or sudden movement occurs, you jump?

All these activities help us to escape from the mundane and enter a world of carefree adventure and enjoyment;

they are great stress busters. We all need rest and relaxation, where we can feel free of our everyday constraints and truly be ourselves from time to time.

Of course, a reminder at this point: if during these activities, or at the end, you should feel guilty, or a thought pops into your mind saying, "its wrong to be doing this when I've got so much else to do" or "I should be at work earning money", then as soon as you accept them, you lose what you've just created. Rather than feeding your positive self-image and feeling happy, you immediately give power to your negative self-image and it's likely you'll feel unhappy, or riddled with guilt or angst.

But logically, however you choose to express yourself, it is okay as long as it's not harmful to yourself or others. If you can accept your behaviour you are creating esteem through self-love.

If you believe you have lots of problems then it may be necessary to explain to people around you that you will have less time for them in the short term. This is something you need to do for you. Once you are out of your rut you will be able to make yourself available to them again at a level appropriate to you both. You are not helping anyone if you are sick and/or unhappy.

So turn to yourself and batten down the hatches. If your lifestyle leaves little opportunity for you, then do the best you can. The most important thing is to make a commitment to yourself to spend more time for your own self-expression and to see it as healthy and positive.

You should remember also the importance of being your best friend and not your worst enemy. This attitude allows you to create a positive connection to self, whatever you are doing.

SEVEN – THE UNIVERSAL MANDATE; YOUR PASSPORT TO FREEDOM

Up to now in this book you have read that the key to finding true happiness lies in learning to love yourself by expressing and accepting; prioritising your various personal obligations; and making sure you set aside some time each day just for you. You have also read about the role played by your attitudes, particularly the self-destructive ones which you may at times acquire from others; but you may still be finding it difficult to implement the necessary changes to your lifestyle.

To help you with this I have developed the Universal Mandate; it is a collection of rights and ideals which allows you to free yourself from unhelpful attitudes and gives you the authority to freely and fairly express yourself. It is your passport to being you.

The Universal Mandate states:

- We are all derived from the same source
- We all have the same right to express our own opinions

- We all have Universal Human Rights
- We all have the right of Political Awareness

We are all derived from the same source

This statement provides a level playing field for humanity. In a purely physical sense we are merely a collection of cells that are arranged into functional organs, tissue, muscles, nerves etc. We all come into this world the same way and we all go out of it the same way. We are born, we exist and we die. This process is a certainty and happens to all of us irrespective of our nationality or social status; there is no escape. It is therefore common to all of us and this is why it can be used as a yardstick.

It follows that, if we are all basically the same, then we must all have the same right to exist on this planet. But if this is so, why doesn't it always feel like that? As Human beings, the differences that exist between us occur during the living part; the bit between the beginning and end of our lives. In the majority of cases our perceived differences stem from our social status.

Status is a reflection of the material world. Money, power, prestige and worth are all material attributes. These energies provide us with material knowledge of who we are in society and where we rank in it.

The business tycoon or successful pop star may have material wealth but this does not afford them a direct right to be emotionally happy; this is why in our Agenda for Living work is only a commitment. The way I see it, you've only truly 'made it' when you can love and accept yourself and reflect this image into the world; it has nothing to do with how wealthy you are.

Remember the story of the Emperors new clothes? Basically, the Emperor only had ears for his views and opinions, which he expected his subjects to reflect back; he surrounded himself with 'yes men' who always affirmed his opinions. This society was very rigid in structure and relied heavily on status and position. This is because, if you can't express your own views, the next best thing is to gain a position as close to the ruler as possible and express his views. This brings you patronage from the ruler and respect from subjects perceived to be below you. People will respect you because of your status with the ruler of the society.

In this society, the Emperor sowed the seeds of his own destruction though, because if everyone always agrees with you, it builds your ego to such a degree you actually start to believe that everybody is telling you the truth, rather than what you want to hear. This left the Emperor open to a clever person who used flattery to deceive. This person flattered the ego of the Emperor and led him to believe he looked magnificent in 'clothes' that did not exist. When the Emperor paraded his new clothes in front of his subjects, they could of course see no clothes and only a naked Emperor.

This fable shows how society 'dresses' people up with status, and this can then be abused to treat people differently. But if you remember this part of the universal mandate, we are all derived from the same source; so even if another person has more money than you, a better job, takes more holidays, and is very charitable, it does not mean they are more human than you are. They are no better than you. Conversely, if most other people have less money and material possessions than you, it does not mean they are less human than you are, and you are no better than them.

A self-loving Awarer attitude is to say it's fine to have material possessions and be financially successful; but they should never be your reason for living, else they will define who you are. Money is best viewed as a vehicle for self-expression in the sense that it provides opportunities to you in life to do and buy things. If you should love money, it is because it helps you to express yourself, rather than simply for itself.

The Universal Mandate sees everybody as a very important person (VIP), because we all have the gift of humanity. Our gift is to be able to express love for ourselves and to the world about us, irrespective of status and money – ultimately it is this attitude that brings happiness. This is the true level playing field, because it allows you to see past the limitations of material status and therefore enhances the development of your humanity.

'We are all derived from the same source' means we are all equal, unless you choose to make it another way.

We all have the same right to express our own opinions

Living is far more than just the physical state of existing. Existing is merely being a living, breathing organism, attempting to survive in its environment; but being alive means you are aware of your identity and have absolute freedom in expressing this knowledge into our physical world.

When you express an opinion, it is a reflection of your self-image. You speak to another with the knowledge of who you are. If they express their own opinion back to you, you may acknowledge its merit but your own sense of identity will enable you to see if it is right for you. If it is you may adopt part or all of their suggestion into your thinking. They may also be receptive to your opinions and together you work in harmony along side one another. In this scenario, each person takes responsibility for expressing their own self-image and accepting this, while also being available to receive opinions from each other and relying upon their own identity to judge its acceptability to them. From this, closer bonds may be formed and both may know themselves as equals, expressing themselves and accepting each other.

Of course, conflict can arise if both parties have very strong but conflicting opinions. In this case the Awarer attitude would be to 'agree to disagree' and move on to another topic, neither party trying to force their opinion onto the other.

It probably goes without saying, that if environments do not allow for free expression, opinion making and therefore the formation of attitudes and ideas will become restricted. In these cases, through implied or real threat, people tailor their self expression to fit in with the prevailing opinion which they know will be accepted.

Fortunately, even if your environment does deny you free expression, you still have the relationship with yourself to fall back on. Even in the direst of circumstances you can always choose to rely on your self-relationship to create love. I remember seeing a story on television, of how Nelson Mandela kept his spirits up during his solitary confinement on Robben Island. Each day, he would turn his attention to tending a small flower in the exercise yard.

You'd have to ask him how it helped, but I would imagine this, and probably other small details, were enough for him to maintain a positive outlook in what were no doubt intimidatory circumstances.

We all have Universal Human Rights

I felt the easiest way to explain this was to discuss the United Nations Universal Declaration of Human Rights (1948). The mandates contained within the various Articles of the declaration work at both a personal and national level. Written after the horrors of World War Two, it was an attempt by the United Nations to see beyond the restrictions of nationalism by joining people together in a common humanitarian purpose. The onus was, and still is, upon member states to create conditions within their countries where a new human spirit of co-operation and peace can be fostered.

The United Nations Declaration of Human Rights gave a blueprint for how citizens could value and respect each other through the protection of economic, political, religious and social rights, and it encouraged member nations to introduce these ideals into their societies. The idea being, if nations co-operate together at a level that is beyond their narrow self-interest, then you can create a 'universal family' of nation states working along side each other in harmony. This leads to less racial intolerance, and consequently there is less chance of conflict and national rivalries.

The above position can also be translated from a national to a personal level. If we feel threatened by our neighbours, then we create defensive emotional attitudes that will help us fight them, if need be. If we feel safe because we share mutual interests, then we will feel easier able to express peaceful attitudes of love for ourselves and others, thus reflecting and realising the true nature and potential of humanity. Given that modern societies appear to be freer than in the past and that 'Universalism' has encouraged many nations to co-operate together in peaceful coexistence, then it must follow that people now have an opportunity to be happier than ever before.

I have reproduced the United Nations Declaration of Human Rights, in Appendix I, because I believe its universal ideals are common to all of humanity and lay down defining principles that assist in our self-acceptance. Moreover, you will have probably heard of it, but have you read it? I hadn't until writing this Book.

We all have the right of Political Awareness

The Universal right of self-acceptance is available to us all, if we choose to exercise it. If human rights help to create an environment where we can more easily express ourselves and create self-love, then political correctness has become the vehicle that allows us to turn this self-knowledge outwards and accept others too. Political correctness is an ideal that was born from the awareness of our human rights and so to understand it further, we must look back over its history.

The Universal Declaration of Human Rights spawned a raft of legislation in member countries that created environments where people could choose to live in peace with each other. This was especially so in western liberal democracies. Across the western world in the 1960's, great social changes also occurred that led to the relaxation of people's attitudes towards sex, marriage, gay relationships, and sexual equality. This produced legislation in that decade, and also in the 1970's, where equitable human rights became enshrined in law. Laws were passed to promote sexual equality, gay rights and racial equality. The idea behind it was that there should be no second-class citizens in society, because everybody deserves first class treatment, irrespective of whoever they may be.

It was in these conditions that what we now know as 'political correctness' developed, becoming apparent as an entity in the 1980's. Its prominence increased throughout the 90's and now in this new millennium it is probably more influential than ever.

The Concise Oxford Dictionary (Ninth Edition) describes political correctness as, "the avoidance of forms of expression or action that exclude, marginalize, or insult certain racial or cultural groups". I feel certain that the scope of political correctness could be widened to also include other minorities and groups within society. I also believe that this should apply in a universal sense, not just from a majority to a minority point of view.

Political correctness seeks to encourage behaviour that reflects the legal requirement that we do not discriminate against minority groups in society. 'Correctness' implies that, unless you behave according to the Law, you shall be in breech of it through 'incorrectness' and then subject to possible prosecution and punishment. The law remains the level playing field, but I believe we can all make a jump to the next level if we change 'correctness' to read 'awareness.'

My reasoning is this; 'correctness' is choosing to express yourself according to a legal mandate, upon which your behaviour will be judged as either right or wrong, whether you like it or not. Because it is legally enforceable and common to all, this standard of behaviour can be said to be a base level. To my mind, 'awareness,' describes understanding the relevance of your behaviour in relation to your circumstances and then choosing to behave appropriately. This standard of behaviour is voluntary and based upon free will, and so by expressing yourself in this way you are promoted immediately to a level above 'correctness'. If you like, you are choosing to express yourself with your heart because this is what you believe;

rather than with your head because this is how you have been told to behave.

By amalgamating Political Correctness and Self Awareness to produce Political Awareness, both ideals can be encompassed together. This interpretation would lead me to define political awareness as being aware of our responsibilities towards other people, whoever they are, by encouraging us to behave in a mutually and universally accepting way. In this scenario, political awareness then becomes a principle for how we treat other people, whether they are of a different race, religion or sexual orientation, the opposite sex, those poorer or richer than us. It means treating people with the dignity and respect they are entitled to as human beings. Through honouring this principle, at a stroke you free yourself from a great deal of hateful prejudice, bigotry, jealousy and envy; the effect of which provides an opportunity to create positive attitudes in your life.

The scope of Political Awareness is therefore greater than Political Correctness, because our participation is not dependent upon us solely recognising the equal opportunities of minorities. Instead it encourages us to treat all people equitably, whoever they may be. This sets a standard that encourages inclusiveness rather than exclusiveness. It makes us aware of our behaviour towards other people and ourselves, while retaining our ability to express and accept.

This brings us full circle, because if we are expressing and accepting, we are creating self-acceptance and love.

Taken as a whole, the universal mandate contains all the necessary strands of human understanding you need to freely express yourself. At its heart is the understanding that you are equal to all others and it is on this basis that it becomes easier to self-accept. If this is good enough for you, then it should also be the same for other people.

CONCLUSION

I hope you've enjoyed reading this Book. I hope it has helped you discover more about yourself, and given you some food for thought.

A lot of what I've written, you probably know anyway. However, putting into practise the things we know we should be doing for ourselves isn't easy; if it was we'd all be doing it and there wouldn't be any problems in the world!

It is easier to ignore our needs than to battle for them, but life becomes so much easier the minute we decide to turn to ourselves with love and acceptance. Despite what we may feel and believe, the authority to choose how we live our lives and how we express ourselves lies solely with us. It's not cloud cuckoo land; self-love is real and available for all, it just takes courage to choose it for ourselves.

It's all about you; so turn to you and take the first step on the road to self-acceptance and ultimately enlightenment.

Appendix I - The United Nations Universal Declaration of Human Rights

Universal Declaration of Human Rights (1948) Preamble.

Whereas recognition of the inherent dignity and of the equal and inalienable rights of all members of the human family is the foundation of freedom, justice and peace in the world,

Whereas disregard and contempt for human rights have resulted in barbarous acts which have outraged the conscience of mankind, and the advent of a world in which human beings shall enjoy freedom of speech and belief from fear and want has been proclaimed as the highest aspiration of the common people,

Whereas it is essential, if man is not to be compelled against tyranny and oppression, that human rights should be protected by the rule of law,

Whereas it is essential to promote the development of friendly relations between nations,

Whereas the peoples of the United Nations have in the Charter reaffirmed their faith in fundamental human rights, in the dignity and worth of the human person and in the equal rights of men and women and have determined to promote social progress and better standards of life in larger freedom,

Whereas Member States have pledged themselves to achieve, in co-operation with the United Nations, the promotion of universal respect for and observance of human rights and fundamental freedoms,

Whereas a common understanding of these rights and freedoms is of the greatest importance for the full realisation of this pledge,

Now, therefore,

The General Assembly

Proclaims this Universal Declaration of Human Rights as a common standard of achievement for all people and all nations, to the end that every individual and ever organ of society, keeping the declaration constantly in mind, shall strive by teaching and education to promote respect for these rights and freedoms and by progressive measures, national and international. To secure their universal and effective recognition and observance, both among the peoples and territories under their jurisdiction.

Article 1

All human beings are born free and equal in dignity and rights. They are endowed with reason and conscience and should act towards one another in a spirit of brotherhood.

Article 2

Everyone is entitled to all the rights and freedoms set forth in this Declaration, without distinction of any kind, such as race, colour, sex, language, religion, political or other opinion, national or social origin, property, birth or other status.

Furthermore, no distinction shall be made on the basis of the political, jurisdictional or international status of the country or territory to which a person belongs, whether it be independent, trust, non self-governing or under any other limitation of sovereignty.

Article 3

Everyone has the right to life, liberty and the security of person.

Article 4

No one shall be in slavery or servitude: slavery and the slave trade shall be prohibited in all their forms.

Article 5

No one shall be subjected to torture or to cruel, inhuman or degrading treatment or punishment.

Article 6

Everyone has the right to recognition everywhere as a person before the law.

Article 7

All are equal before the law and are entitled without any discrimination to equal protection of the law. All are entitled to equal protection against any discrimination in violation of this Declaration and against any incitement to such discrimination.

Article 8

Everyone has the right to an effective remedy by the competent national tribunals for acts violating the fundamental rights granted him by the constitution or by law.

Article 9

No one shall be subjected to arbitrary arrest, detention or exile.

Article 10

Everyone is entitled in full equality to a fair, and public hearing by an independent and impartial tribunal, in the determination of his rights and obligations and of any criminal charge against him

Article 11

1. Everyone charged with a penal offence has the right to be presumed innocent until proved guilty according to law in a public trial at which he has had all the guarantees necessary for his defence.

2. No one shall be held guilty of any penal offence on account of any act or omission which did not constitute a penal offence, under national or international law, at the time when it was committed. Nor shall a heavier penalty be imposed than the one that was applicable at the time the penal offence was committed.

Article 12

No one shall be subjected to arbitrary interference with his privacy, family, home or correspondence, nor to attacks upon his honour and reputation. Everyone has the right to the protection of the law against such interference or attacks.

Article 13

1. Everyone has the right to freedom of movement and residence within the borders of each State.

2. Everyone has the right to leave any country, including his own, and to return to his country.

Article 14

1. Everyone has the right to seek and to enjoy in other countries asylum from persecution.

2 This right may not be invoked in the case of prosecutions genuinely arising from non-political crimes or from acts contrary to the purposes and principles of the United Nations.

Article 15

1. Everyone has the right to a nationality.

2. No one shall be deprived of his nationality nor denied the right to change his nationality.

Article 16

1. Men and women of full age, without any limitation due to race, nationality or religion, have the right to marry and to found a family. They are entitled to equal rights as to marriage, during marriage and at its dissolution.

2. Marriage shall be entered into only with the free and full consent of the intending spouses.

3. The family is the natural and fundamental group unit of society and is entitled to protection by society and the State.

Article 17

1. Everyone has the right to own property alone as well as in association with others.

2. No one shall be arbitrarily deprived of his property.

Article 18

Everyone has the right to freedom of thought, conscience and religion; this right includes freedom to change his religion or belief, and freedom, either alone or in community with others and in public or private, to manifest his religion or belief in teaching, practice, worship and observance.

Article 19

Everyone has the right to freedom of opinion and expression; this includes freedom to hold opinions without interference and to seek, receive and impart information and ideas through any media and regardless of frontiers.

Article 20

1. Everyone has the right to freedom of peaceful assembly and association.

2. No one may be compelled to belong to an association.

Article 21

1 Everyone has the right to take part in the government of his country, directly or through freely chosen representatives.

2 Everyone has the right of equal access to public service in his country.

3 The will of the people shall be the basis of the authority of government; this shall be expressed in periodic and genuine elections which shall be by universal and equal suffrage and shall be held by secret vote or by equivalent free voting procedures.

Article 22

Everyone, as a member of society, has the right to social security and is entitled to realisation, through national effort and international co-operation and in accordance with the organisation and resources of each State, of the economic, social and cultural rights indispensable for his dignity and the free development of his personality.

Article 23

1. Everyone has the right to work, to free choice of employment, to just and favourable conditions of work and to protection against unemployment.

2. Everyone, without any discrimination, has the right to equal pay for equal work.

3. Everyone who works has the right to just and favourable remuneration ensuring for himself and his family an existence worthy of human dignity, and supplemented, if necessary by other means of social protection.

4. Everyone has the right to form and to join trade unions for the protection of his interests.

Article 24

Everyone has the right to rest and leisure, including reasonable limitation of working hours and periodic holidays with pay.

Article 25

1. Everyone has the right to a standard of living adequate for the health and well-being of himself and his family, including food, clothing, housing and medical care and necessary social services, and the right to security in the event of unemployment sickness, disability, widowhood, old age or other lack of livelihood in circumstances beyond his control.

2. Education shall be directed to the full development of the human personality and to the strengthening of respect for human rights and fundamental freedoms. It shall promote among all nations, racial or religious groups, and shall further the

activities of the United Nations for the maintenance of peace.

3. Parents have a prior right to choose the kind of education that shall be given to their children.

Article 27

1. Everyone has the right to participate in the cultural life of the community, to enjoy the arts and to share in scientific advancement and its benefits.

2 Everyone has the right to the protection of the moral and material interests resulting from any scientific, literary or artistic production of which he is the author.

Article 28

Everyone is entitled to a social and international order in which the rights and freedoms set forth in this Declaration can be fully realized.

Article 29

1. Everyone has duties to the community in which alone the free and full development of his personality is possible.

2. In the exercise of his rights and freedoms, everyone shall be subject only to such limitations as are determined by law solely for the purpose of securing due recognition and respect for the rights and freedoms of others and of meeting the just requirements of morality, public order and the general welfare in a democratic society.

3. These rights and freedoms may in no case be exercised contrary to the purposes and principles of the United Nations.

Article 30

Nothing in this Declaration may be interpreted as implying for any State, group or person any right to engage in any activity or perform any act aimed at the destruction of any of the rights and freedoms set forth herein.

Acknowledgements

All dictionary definitions used in this Book were taken from The Concise Oxford Dictionary (Ninth Edition)

United Nations Declaration of Human Rights reproduced with the kind permission of the UN.